I'll Fix That Cat Later!

Brenda Short

Library and Archives Canada Cataloguing in Publication

ISBN 978-1-0691107-0-1 (pbk)

Short, Brenda, author

I'll Fix That Cat Later! / Brenda Short

Illustrated by Microsoft AI

Published by Doonhamer Publishing 2024

Dedication

Dedicated to my grandchildren.

Children's books by this author

1. The Cherry Pie Incident
2. Noel and Sherlock
3. I'll Fix That Cat Later!
4. The Christmas Surprise
5. Frank's My Name
6. The Fishing Trip
7. The Empty Nest
8. Easter Bunny Has a Fever

Preface

These are the adventures of Blossom, a small Cairn Terrier, with her friends, the house cat, the mailman, the neighbour's new dog Max and of course, her beloved Teddy.

Chapter 1 - Blossom

Blossom opened her eyes, her head popping up suddenly like a jack-in-the-box, and looked around the room. Her nose twitched as she sniffed the air.

There was a distinct smell of cat, but that wasn't unusual. Apart from that, she smelled nothing alarming.

Everything was quiet now…so quiet she could hear a pin drop. Nothing assailed her ears, except her own sniffing sounds, but…she had definitely heard something a moment ago. Some comings or goings or other such nonsense. That's what had awakened her from a sound sleep.

"Teddy!" she whimpered, panicking suddenly, and searching the far reaches of her wicker basket.

Was there some terrible plot to kidnap him? Would he be held for ransom?

She could offer a half-chewed marrow bone for his return. There was still plenty of flavour left on it.

Now, where did she put the bone?

Almost immediately, her fears were dismissed. There he was, her bosom buddy sitting at the front door, quite beaten up but still loveable, although looking quite sad.

Teddy was her absolute all-time, favourite toy, despite being in a sad state.

She had accidentally shaken his ear loose last year and she had apologized to Teddy many times for this transgression… but only in her mind of course.

His nose was all chewed up as well, but she was not the one who was responsible for his deformity. This was down to her nemesis the cat, who lived here too.

Blossom looked up just in time to see a black tail disappear around the kitchen door, but she was still half asleep.

First she had to stretch and yawn. She would fix that cat…later!

So, when she had finished yawning and stretching, her usual aerobics loosely based on yoga, it was time and off she went on her mission to find him.

Her first stop...the kitchen. All the bowls were empty!

"No food, no water…where does he put it all? How big is his stomach anyway?" she muttered, forgetting that she herself had emptied them last night.

She had licked the food bowls clean of the last remnants of supper, and the water bowl completely dry, with no consideration that the cat might need water too.

"That cat eats as much as an elephant," Blossom muttered again, although she wasn't sure how much an elephant ate.

She sniffed at her empty bowl, "It's time for action."

She ran through the house and bounded up onto her human's bed.

"Wake up!...wake up!" Blossom
squeaked and barked.

Mrs. Adams was sound asleep,
blowing little raspberries and dreaming
about making cupcakes, until her little friend
started to lick her face, barking loudly.

"Good morning, Blossom! What's wrong?" she said, throwing off the bedcovers.

"Do you need to go pee? Are you hungry, pet? Okay, let me get up and I'll feed you."

Mrs. Adams was a kind person and Blossom loved her very much. There was a quiet air about her that always calmed the excitable Blossom.

"Did that naughty cat eat your food again?" she cooed lovingly, tickling Blossom gently behind the ears.

Was there any question about it? Of course, the cat ate her food.

He was as big as an elephant! But she would catch up with him later.

After breakfast, she went into the garden to sniff around. First, down to the fence to look for the mailman.

He should be here soon, and he always gave her a cookie and tickled behind her ears…

Once she saw a mouse here and chased it for hours.

Well actually, it was gone in a second, zig zagging into the tall grass, but it was fun while it lasted, and she had spent the next while sniffing the area and pretending to chase it.

"No mouse…and no mailman!" she thought. "Maybe the cat ate both of them, after all he's as big as an elephant.

"Where could he be? Probably visiting someone else's house and eating their breakfast too. Oh well! He'll turn up eventually. I'll fix that cat later!"

Chapter 2 - The Mailman

Next day was just like any other day. Blossom woke bright and early, checked on Teddy…he was in the corner of the basket…then jumped on the bed beside her human, Mrs. Adams and proceeded to lick her on the nose.

Blossom was hungry and was looking forward to her breakfast. Mrs. Adams filled the dog bowl with nutritious food and replenished the water too.

As soon as Blossom finished eating, Mrs. Adams opened the back door and let the dog out.

Blossom went into the garden to sniff around, and check for intruders.

She took Teddy outside with her, shaking him furiously until his ear almost came off, and then dropped him onto the porch steps.

She would play with him later, but first, down to the fence to look for the mailman.

Mr. Mailman should be along any minute now and he always gave her a cookie and a pat on the head. Such a nice man…

Once she saw a mouse here and chased it for hours! Well, actually it was more like a moment or two.

It zig-zagged like a lightening bolt, and then was gone in a second, but it was fun while it lasted.

Where was that fat cat anyway?

He must be up to no good! Blossom hadn't seen him yet this morning, which meant that he had been out all night again and wasn't in a hurry to come home.

Someone must be feeding him!

He certainly had a way with him,
swaggering up and down the street, his long
fluffy tail switching from side to side, and
all the neighbours just loving him, especially
when he wrapped himself around their legs,
purring loudly.

Blossom waited patiently, but the street was empty, and quiet…just as empty as the garden.

"No mouse…no mailman," she thought, disappointedly. "Maybe the cat ate both of them? One of these days I'll fix that cat!"

Suddenly, she could hear whistling in the distance. It was the mailman…he was coming…yay!

She ran up and down the length of the fence, barking excitedly, in anticipation of the treat and a tickle behind the ears from her mailman.

"Here's my favourite girl! Hello Blossom," he said pleasantly setting down his heavy bag of mail to rub her ears and give her the cookie treat.

Blossom preened. She was his favourite!

He was very fond of this little dog. Other dogs seemed to be angry when he came with the mail and growled at him, sometimes snapping at him too, but Blossom was always friendly and took the cookie gently in the most ladylike manner, not grabbing it from his fingers.

She wasn't hungry, as she had just finished breakfast, but ate the treat anyway, wagging her tail and licking his hand to show her appreciation.

She had good manners…not like that pesky cat!

Soon, the mailman was on his way. She followed him along the length of the fence, watched him put letters in the heavy, tin mailbox, then go on to the next house.

The neighbour's dog was waiting for him too and barked and barked. There was a noticeable absence of good breeding, but was that because it was a mutt?

Most mixed breeds had impeccable manners, but this dog had no manners at all, and snapped and snarled at the mailman as he tried to give it a treat. Too bad!

But what was that? Something was moving in the grass, just where she had eaten the cookie. The mouse was back!

It had sneaked back into the garden to feast on the crumbs that she dropped as she crunched her way through the cookie treat.

She had to be more elegant when she ate.

Mrs. Adams wouldn't want mice in the house, but wasn't that what cats were for – keeping mice out?

Where was that big furball when you needed him?

    She had to act quickly. It was there for
the crumbs, but it saw her coming and
disappeared in a flash, zigzagging towards
the tall grass as Blossom ran back to the
spot.

Just at that moment, who should saunter in through a hole in the fence, but him…Mrs. Adam's obnoxious cat, licking his lips lasciviously?

He had just finished breakfast from the person next door. He was so fickle and visited all the neighbours in turn, looking for food. No wonder he was as big as an elephant.

Blossom knew right away that he had been next door, because they always fed him canned cat food and Blossom could smell that disgusting fishy breath as he swaggered towards her.

"Can't have him smelling the place up," she decided, "or me either!

She didn't want him to start licking his fishy tongue all over her as he usually did when he finished eating.

First, he would clean his paws and face and then start on Blossom, cleaning her eyes and ears.

But then unfortunately, she would smell of fish all day. Better to chase him away before he began his cleaning routine.

So, she began to bark and ran towards him menacingly.

The cat took off hissing and spitting and ran up a tree, loving the attention.

Blossom unfortunately couldn't climb the tree, but stayed at the bottom for several moments, paws as far up the trunk as she could manage and barking a warning to the cat.

The cat decided to stay up the tree, actually finding it difficult to climb back down again.

He had visited two of his breakfast haunts and had eaten at both, so he was so full he could burst.

He was as big as an elephant!

Eventually, he fell asleep in the warmth of the early morning sunshine, laying across the largest branch.

"He'll come down eventually," thought Blossom, deciding to play with Teddy in the meantime. "Can't stay up there forever, can he! I'll fix that cat later!"

Chapter 3 – Max

Next morning, Blossom had just finished her breakfast and had wandered outside with Teddy when she heard voices and barking at the bottom of the garden.

What was all that noise, coming from the other side of the hedge? Was there a dog over there? Yes! Blossom could hear lots of barking and the Browns were there too, laughing at something.

She dropped Teddy on the porch steps and ran over to the hedge barking loudly to announce herself, which prompted Mrs. Brown to come over.

"Hi Blossom, please come and play
with Max. I'm quite worn out."

"Who is Max?" Blossom barked.

"I haven't heard of a Max in the neighbourhood. He must be new. Well, if he barks, at least he isn't a cat!"

Mrs. Brown lifted Blossom over the fence and plopped her down in front of the other dog. Max was a small, black puppy, a Scottish terrier.

Blossom looked at Max, and Max looked at Blossom. Then both dogs immediately began sniffing the other all over.

Max began yapping and running all around like a little wind-up toy, so Blossom decided to join in.

Well! They ran up and down and round and round for a few minutes. This was fun!

"It's just like they've been friends forever," said Mrs. Brown, happily.

Finally, the dogs lay down beside each other panting. Mrs. Adams brought a bowl of water from her kitchen and they both drank noisily, then shook their heads, water flying everywhere.

Once their thirst was slaked, they took off running again, up and down the sidewalk and in and out of everyone's legs.

In the meantime, curiosity got the better of the cat and he came out of the garden to the other side of the fence. He needed to see what was happening.

Big mistake on his part!

"Cat!" Max yipped, excitedly.

"I owe him big time. I'll fix that cat!" barked Blossom.

Both dogs charged towards the cat at the same time, tails wagging and ears flapping.

The cat took off, of course, and ran up the nearest tree where he stood on a branch with his back arched, fluffing himself up to look much larger and hissing and spitting loudly.

"That's more like it!" the cat mewed, happily.

"It's about time that dog paid more attention to me. She never plays with me anymore, ever since she got Teddy, but I showed them. I chewed off his nose."

The two dogs and the cat played tag
for a while, but soon it was time for Max to
go home with the Browns.

That night, Blossom and the cat climbed into the big wicker basket and took Teddy with them.

Blossom let the cat lick her face as usual, then he licked Teddy's face, mewing an apology for the nose incident, before they all settled down for the night.

Just before Blossom fell asleep, she turned to her teddy bear and whispered, "It's alright Teddy. I'll fix that cat…tomorrow!"